FOCUS ON THE PROCESS

THE SIMPLE "SECRET" TO ACHIEVING YOUR GOALS

THIBAUT MEURISSE

First published 2026

ISBN 978-81-8328-697-8 (PB); 978-81-8328-699-2 (HB)

Published by
Wisdom Tree
4779/23, Ansari Road
Darya Ganj, New Delhi-110 002
Ph.: 011-23247966/67/68
wisdomtreebooks@gmail.com

Printed in India

CONTENTS

INTRODUCTION

The only way to achieve any goal is to focus on the process.

The process *is* the goal, and the outcome we seek is merely its logical consequence. Yet too often, we forget this simple truth. We don't realize that the process is the only thing we ever have control over. We often fail to recognize that embracing the process is the most effective way to reach our goals. As a result, we look elsewhere for quick fixes, gimmicks, and magic pills. We buy into the next get-rich-quick scheme, try the new fad diet, or download the favored language app of the day. In doing so, we inevitably face disappointment after disappointment.

The purpose of this book is to serve as a reminder that the process is the solution. It is to remind us that by *consistently* focusing on the small actions that matter, we will reach the results we want. Consistency is key—and until we understand it at a deeper level, nothing will work for us.

My hope is that you will refer to this book whenever you forget about the process and start veering off track. Trust me, this will happen many times.

In this book, we will explore what the process is, how it works, and why it is the key to not only reaching our goals, but also to achieving more peace of mind, a deeper focus, and a more meaningful life overall.

In **part I. What the process is and why it matters,** I will provide a definition of "process" and will demonstrate the benefits of focusing on it.

In **part II. How to focus on the process**, we will go over the different components and concepts that go into creating an effective process. Among other things, we will discuss the difference between "process" goals and "result" goals. We will see the importance of starting small, and we will learn what to do when the initial excitement wears off. We will discuss the various pitfalls and traps that people fall into when they try to make the process their goal.

Finally, in **part III. Refining the process,** we will see how to identify the right process based on our goals. We will discuss why it is important to gather feedback early on and stress the importance of building a process that is sustainable in the long term. Then, we will review ways to optimize the process to ensure we reach our goals.

Let us dive in.

YOUR STEP BY STEP WORKBOOK

To help you improve your process, I have created a workbook as a companion guide to this book. Make sure to download it at the following URL:

https://whatispersonaldevelopment.org/workbooks

If you have any difficulties downloading the workbook, contact me at: thibaut.meurisse@gmail.com and I will send it as soon as possible.

Alternatively, you can also use the workbook available at the end of this book.

PART I

WHAT THE PROCESS IS AND WHY IT MATTERS

When we set goals, most of us choose a specific target that we would like to hit. For instance, it could be the amount of money we would like to make, how much weight we would like to lose, or how fast we would like to run a marathon.

Having a well-defined target is an excellent starting point. Few people have clear goals, and the people who have defined goals are probably doing much better than those who don't.

However, the problem comes when we spend too much time and energy focusing on the target. We worry whether we will hit it. We wonder if we are good enough. Or we feel overwhelmed by the enormity of our goal. As a result, we procrastinate, we look for shortcuts, or we give up on our dreams altogether. When we behave this way, we forget about the only thing that truly matters: the process.

Success in any area of our lives is always the result of a process. Nobody wakes up an NBA player, a successful entrepreneur, or a world-class violinist. Successful people all went through a process that required a great deal of time, effort, and consistency. Yet, many of us want to get the process out of the way while forgetting that the process *is* the way. We want to lose weight without changing our lifestyle, make money without working for it, or attract the ideal partner without going on dates. In short, we want the results without working through the process.

It does not work.

It is what we do consistently and deliberately to move us closer toward the achievement of a specific goal that matters. While it may sound obvious, we often fail to grasp this at a deep enough level to transform our lives.

In truth, the process *is* the goal. The process is the way out of lack of success, worries, overthinking, and many other symptoms that result from obsessing over the outcome. The process is how ordinary people become extraordinary—how they achieve results only a minority of people do.

What is the process?

For the sake of this book, I will define the process as:

the daily or weekly activities that, when done consistently, will significantly increase the odds of us reaching our goals.

A straightforward example is a writer who writes every morning consistently for years. By doing so, they put the odds in their favor. Of course, many components play a part in a writer's success, but writing regularly would be a good start. Other examples could be someone who hits the gym consistently for years or a budding pianist who practices daily.

In other words, the process is what we do consistently to reach our desired results. And this is something we have complete control over. When we make the process our focal point, we can achieve goals that may seem unattainable. More specifically, below are the key benefits of focusing on the process rather than on the outcome.

1. **Reduce stress, worry, and sense of overwhelm.** Focusing on the process enables us to stop worrying so much about the end result. It helps us zero in on the task at hand, knowing we are doing the best we can today.

2. **Boost our emotional resilience.** Sometimes, we may struggle to move toward our goals quickly enough. As a result, we may begin to feel disheartened, disappointed, or hopeless. Immersing ourselves in the process will move us back to the present reality and will empower us to focus on what we can do *now*.

3. **Enhance our focus.** Focusing on the process every day consistently conditions our minds and boosts our overall levels of concentration.

4. **Strengthen our self-discipline.** As the self-esteem expert, Nathaniel Branden, wrote, "Self-esteem is the reputation we acquire with ourselves." By sticking to the process, we increase our discipline and improve our sense of self-respect.
5. **Compound our results.** Focusing on the process daily regardless of how we feel enables us to build our skills and make progress.
6. **Put the focus back on ourselves.** Putting our attention on the process enables us to stop comparing ourselves to other people. It helps us let go of the idea that we are falling behind or that we are not good enough. Others are on their journey, and we are on ours. All we need to do is follow the process and trust that we will accomplish *our* goals.

To conclude, the process acts as an anchor. It helps us eliminate unnecessary worries, increase our emotional resilience, boost our focus, strengthen our discipline, and stop comparing ourselves to others. It is our emotional safety net. Therefore, whenever we feel overwhelmed, worry too much, feel scared of doing something, or get distracted, we must focus back on the process.

I used the process to become a successful author, help me

with dating, transform my health, enhance my emotional well-being, and learn multiple foreign languages. And I highly encourage you to use the process to reach your most important goals too.

Remember, the process is the goal—and the outcome we seek is merely its logical conclusion.

* * *

Action step

Select one major goal you have achieved in the past. Then, ask yourself the following questions:

- What was the process that enabled me to reach my goals? What was I doing each day/week?
- What were the benefits? (Look at benefits #1 to #6 in your action guide and see with how much intensity you felt each benefit.

PART II

HOW TO FOCUS ON THE PROCESS

For the process to work for us, we must work at it. That is, we must define the best possible process for any meaningful goal we wish to achieve. Following our process should almost guarantee that we will reach our goals. In this section, let us see how to improve our process and ensure we focus on it consistently.

A. Prioritize process goals over result goals

The most disciplined among us write down the specific goals we would like to achieve. Then, we work toward those goals in the best way possible. Having clear targets is essential, but it is only the first step. The second step is to break them down into smaller tasks. The third step is to put in place the correct and most effective process. And the fourth and final step is to practice detaching ourselves from the outcome.

Or to summarize:

Step 1—Set a clear target

Step 2—Break it down into milestones

Step 3—Put in place the right process

Step 4—Focus on the process

Ultimately, the most powerful stage is to forget about the results and focus on the process (step 4). It is to become one with the process and anchor ourselves in the present moment. Our only goal is to focus on the process today—right here, right now. Therefore, when setting goals, make sure to:

1. choose a specific target (result goal), and

2. design a process to reach it (process goal).

Put simply, the *result* goal is the outcome we want and the *process* goal is what will get us there. Below are examples (suggestions):

- Read forty books in our field this year —> Read for one hour daily

- Learn to play Beethoven's "Fur Elise" —> Practice the piano for two hours every day

- Have a conversation with a Spanish native speaker by year end —> Study Spanish for thirty minutes every day

- Land five new clients this month —> Cold call prospects for two hours each morning

In the end, what we do *consistently* enables us to master any skill and reach any goal. Some of the most skilled people in the world have been practicing their craft daily for years. The Olympic swimmer, Michael Phelps, did not miss a day of training between the age of twelve and eighteen. And the successful writer, Stephen King, still writes every day, seven days a week.

As the journalist, Neil Strauss, wrote, "Success comes down to doing the obvious thing for an uncommonly long period of time without convincing yourself you are smarter than you are." The point is, the best people in their field are masters of processes, maestros of consistency, and virtuosos of repetition. They rely on consistency and patience to attain their goals. They make the process their focal point.

If we want to reach our goals, we must learn to stick to the process for as long as necessary.

* * *

Action step

Using your action guide, select one goal you want to work on. Then, follow steps 1 to 4 below:

Step 1—Set a clear target

Step 2—Break it down into milestones

Step 3—Put in place the right process

Step 4—Focus on the process

B. Understand the cycle of excitement

On paper, focusing on the process is simple. We follow our process each day, whether it is playing an instrument, calling customers, or learning a foreign language. And *voilà*! Success follows.

However, the reality is more complex. While the process requires consistency and regularity, our life is hectic. We may become sick, face issues at work, or encounter problems in our personal lives. Or we may sabotage ourselves because of various fears. If we are not careful, our process will soon be gone. We will have abandoned it, often without even noticing it.

To protect our process, we must understand the typical journey we embark on when pursuing a new venture. I call it "the cycle of excitement".

Let us review this cycle and its various stages.

Stage 1—Initial excitement.

When starting a new endeavor, we usually feel a sense of excitement. We cannot wait to see our progress. So, for a few weeks, or perhaps a few months, we work hard. As a result, we begin to see positive results and we feel good.

Stage 2—Plateau

However, soon enough, we stop seeing such fast progress. It may even seem that we are going backward. Despite following the same process, we don't see improvements. So, we start to doubt ourselves.

Is this working? Why don't I get the results I desire? What is wrong with me?

As a result, we start losing hope, and this is when many people give up.

Stage 3—Breakthrough

In spite of our lack of progress, we decide to trust the process and remain consistent. Suddenly, we have a breakthrough. We notice significant improvements. It is as if we have reached a new level. Our skill levels have improved, and/or we notice tangible results. As a result, we are reinvigorated.

Stage 4—Back to excitement

Having witnessed progress, we experience a renewed sense of excitement which brings us back to stage 1 (initial excitement).

This cycle will usually repeat several times. We will reach plateaus again and again. But we will have to keep trusting the process regardless of our external results (or lack thereof).

Understanding the cycle of excitement is critical. It enables us to identify where we are in the cycle and helps maintain faith in the process. Many people give up too soon, too close to a breakthrough. Don't do the same thing. Push through to success!

However, note that if we fail to reach breakthroughs, our process might be the issue, and if so, it will need to be refined. We will see how to do that in **Part III. Refining the Process.**

* * *

Action step

- Think of a time you entered the cycle of excitement with one of your goals.
- Then, reflect on what happened. Did you keep going? Did you give up?
- What could you have done differently?

C. Develop faith in the process

We often judge ourselves based on our results. We compare ourselves to others and feel discouraged when we fall short. Focusing on the process means forgetting about the results, but also about other people. Where we start is irrelevant. All that matters is that we stick to the process and keep improving. The key is consistency. Our ability to stay consistent over a long period of time will enable us to achieve almost any goal we may imagine.

Therefore, we must assess ourselves based on our level of consistency. Ignore what other people do—or what we did in the past. And, once we set our target, avoid worrying about the future. Focus on the process knowing that, over a long enough timeframe, it will enable us to reach our goals.

* * *

Action step

Answer the following questions in your action guide:

- How much time do I spend worrying about the results?
- How is it helping me to reach my goals?

D. Realize that the process is the goal

Once we understand that our only job is to focus on the process, everything will change for us. We will stop worrying so much about the results. We won't feel overwhelmed by the size of our vision. And we will be less likely to procrastinate. Putting in place an effective process and following it *is* the actual goal. Therefore, whenever we doubt ourselves, lack motivation, or feel scared, we must take a deep breath and refocus on the process.

* * *

Action step

- Take a moment to reflect on the fact that your process will lead you to the achievement of your goals.
- Visualize yourself making progress toward your goals

each day—forever. Ask yourself this question: "If I stay consistent, keep going, and refuse to give up, what will happen in the next six months, twelve months, five years, and ten years?"

E. Clarify your goals

Vague goals lead to vague processes. If we don't know where we are going, how can we discover the best way to get there?

Focusing on the process is the best thing we can ever do, but only if our process is effective. Fortunately, it is often quite straightforward. For instance, if we want to run a marathon, we can easily find an effective training blueprint. After all, many people have run marathons before us. Our blueprint might not be perfect, but as long as we follow the process, stay consistent, and make adjustments as we progress, we will be more likely to reach our goal.

Similarly, if we want to learn how to play the guitar, there are many tutorials online or teachers that can help us in the process. By doing our own research and putting a process in place, we will eventually reach our goal.

The same goes for learning foreign languages. There is a degree of uncertainty. How long it will take will vary from one person to the next, but if we are consistent enough, we will make progress, and we will succeed.

The bottom line is, for any goal, we can identify an effective process that will help us reach it. And the clearer our goal is, the easier it will be to achieve it.

* * *

Action step

- Revisit your previous goal in *A. Prioritize process goals over result goals.*
- Now, how could you make it even more specific and create a better process?

F. Start small

Once we have identified a clear goal, we should start small. Tiny actions performed consistently for a long period of time can generate enormous momentum and lead to extraordinary results.

Walk for five minutes. Do ten pushups.

Write one paragraph. Learn five words in Italian.

Just get started. The initial level of intensity does not matter. What matters is the level of consistency. Once we have learned to maintain a habit for a reasonably long period of time, it will have a ripple effect on many areas of our life. We will feel more confident. We will trust ourselves and our abilities more and more. And, over time, we will feel the desire to set bigger and more ambitious goals.

We all have to start somewhere. And starting small is better than not starting at all.

* * *

Action step

Answer the following question using your action guide:

- If I were to do them consistently for six months, which small action(s) would enable me to make continual progress toward my goals?

G. Make consistency part of our identity

Consistency and discipline are habits. As we practice focusing on the process, it will transform us into one of the most disciplined persons we will ever meet.

When I decided to pursue ambitious goals, one of my first decisions was to create a morning routine. I stuck to it diligently for over six months without missing a day. It enabled me to develop confidence and, little by little, build the identity of a high achiever.

What matters most is how we view ourselves. The subjective reality that we see for ourselves is far more important than the "objective" reality others see for us. In other words, what matters most is not what people think we can do, but what *we* think we can do. And it all starts by upgrading our identity.

When we fail to reach our goals, it is often because of an identity issue, not a capability issue. Consistency is what enables us to build the new identity needed to reach our goals. So, focus on the process *every day*. Start with a thirty-day challenge. Then, extend it to ninety days, six months, one year, five years. This will boost our self-confidence and allow us to supercharge our results. Over time, we will feel compelled to tackle bigger goals, and we will build unstoppable momentum.

Ultimately, we don't usually become extraordinary by doing extraordinary things—but by doing *ordinary* things with *extraordinary* consistency.

* * *

Action step

- Make consistency part of your identity. Think of consistency as part of who you are. Tell yourself that you are someone who is extremely consistent. You keep focusing on the process until you reach your goals.
- Adopt the following mantra: "I keep going until I reach my goals. It is just who I am." (Alternatively, come up with your own mantra.)

H. Commit to a thirty-day challenge

Whenever I wish to adopt a new habit, I start a thirty-day challenge. I take a pen and a sheet of paper and draw a vertical line for each day I stick to my habit.

I encourage you to try thirty-day challenges too. And once you reach thirty days, consider extending the period to ninety days. Or if you realize there is a better habit you would like to adopt instead, switch the habit and restart the challenge.

* * *

Action step

- Revisit your previous goal.
- Then, select one habit you will stick to for the next thirty days as part of your challenge.

I. Practice self-compassion

Self-compassion is the glue that makes consistency possible. It is the safety net that enables us to keep going when we feel like giving up. While the process is the goal, self-compassion is the guardrail that prevents us from going off track and abandoning our process.

The point is this. Consistency requires self-compassion. People often give up on their goals because they lose motivation or hope. It happens because of constant negative self-talk and unrealistic expectations. Remember, worrying about the outcome won't help. And plateaus and lack of progress are to be expected along the journey.

Now, here are a few tips to help develop more self-compassion:

1. Let go of myths around self-compassion

People struggle to be kind to themselves because they cling to a distorted view of self-compassion.

First, we believe that being self-compassionate is selfish. We think, "Who am I to think of myself first and talk to myself in a kind and encouraging way? There are so many people I need to be kind to before I can be kind to myself."

Second, we believe that being kind to ourselves is a sign of weakness. "If I am too kind to myself, it will make me weak."

Third, we assume that being self-compassionate will make us complacent. "If I don't beat myself up, I won't get anything done."

But none of these myths are true.

As we cultivate self-compassion, we will feel better about ourselves, and we will have more emotional room to be there for others. We will also be able to bounce back quickly from challenges and stay consistent. Like a reed, we will bend, but we won't break. Finally, we will realize that we get significantly more done when we stop criticizing ourselves.

Practice being kind to yourself so that you can stay focused on the process and reach your goals. It will change your life.

2. Monitor your self-talk

We have discussed the myths around self-compassion. Now, let us see how we can be more self-compassionate.

The first step is to become mindful of our self-talk. How are we talking to ourselves during a typical day? Are we encouraging ourselves, or are we criticizing ourselves whenever we make a mistake?

The second step is to practice noticing when we are being overly harsh with ourselves. Without awareness, we won't be able to improve our self-talk. If we struggle to monitor our internal monologue, we will fail to notice when we experience unpleasant emotional states such as guilt, shame, anger, or frustration. Often, the way we feel is influenced by the words we use when talking to ourselves. When we observe our feelings, we will start uncovering the content of our inner conversation.

3. Update our self-talk

The last step is to update our self-talk. It will require practice, but it is worth it. Years ago, I decided to stop disrespecting myself. I practiced reformulating any statement I perceived as an insult to myself until it became a habit. Below are a few examples:

What did I do? I am so stupid.

—> I wish I had done things differently, but I made a mistake. And it is okay. I will be more careful next time.

Everything I do sucks. Why can't I be better at what I do?

—> I am not at the level I want to be yet, and it is okay. I will keep learning and improving.

Why does it always happen to me?

—> Sometimes, bad things happen to me, but bad things happen to everyone. And I am also lucky on many occasions.

We must make sure to practice reformulating how we talk to ourselves. It will be one of the most useful things we will ever do to support ourselves.

* * *

Action step

1. Reassess your belief around self-compassion and let go of the following myths:

   Myth #1. Self-compassion is selfish

   Myth #2. Being kind to myself is a sign of weakness

   Myth #3. Self-compassion will make me lazy

2. Monitor your self-talk

   This week, pay extra attention to the way you talk to yourself. Write down in your action guide, what you say to yourself in the following instances:

   - When you make a mistake
   - When something does not go as planned
   - When you experience negative emotions such as frustration, anger, jealousy, or sadness

3. Update your self-talk

    - Write down what you want to say to yourself when you are struggling emotionally

    - Go back to your previous examples and write down what you will tell yourself instead next time a similar thing happens.

PART III

REFINING THE PROCESS

The more effective our process is, the more likely we are to reach our goals. In this part, we will review what we can do to refine our process.

The illusion of the perfect process

The first thing to understand is that the perfect process seldom exists. Our process cannot guarantee one hundred percent that we will reach our goals, no matter how consistent we may be. That is the sad reality of life. But that is also what keeps it interesting. There is always an element of uncertainty.

The beauty of having an effective process is that it reduces uncertainty while improving the odds of success. Our process might not be perfect, but if we want to reach our biggest goals, we need it to be as good as it can possibly be.

Identifying the right process

Some goals are straightforward; others are complicated and require extensive study to figure out the right process.

Earlier, we saw that writing each day consistently was a good start if we wish to become a full-time author. Unfortunately, this does not always guarantee success. Perhaps we write in a niche with little to no audience. Perhaps, we attempt to create a masterpiece even though we have never written anything before. Or, perhaps, we keep writing, hoping to improve our craft. In short, the process is suboptimal, and the strategy is unlikely to work.

The bottom line is, the process is not just what we do consistently, but also *how* we do it. Consistency can go a long way, but sometimes it is not enough. As a rule of thumb, the more the odds are stacked against us, the more we should strive to identify the most effective process. To do so, we must:

1. **Learn as much as we can about our goal**. The more we know about our goals, the easier it will be to identify the best process to reach them.

2. **Be willing to commit long term.** The more consistent we are, the more we activate the power of compounding, and the more we will increase the odds of attaining our goals.

3. **Seek honest feedback.** The more feedback we receive,

the more data we have to refine our process. Feedback lets us know if we are heading in the right direction or if we are veering off track.

Remember that a challenging goal leaves little room for error and may require luck (at least in the short term). That is why we must design the best strategy possible.

In summary, a good process is a one that is likely to lead us to the desired outcome. Now, here is a great question to assess the quality of the process:

"If I keep doing what I am doing today or this week, will I achieve my goal?"

If what we do today or this week will *not* allow us to be where we would like to be in five or ten years, we will have to change something.

* * *

Action step

- Revisit your previous goals
- Now, using your action guide, rate yourself on the three points below:

1. I learn everything I can about my goals
2. I am willing to commit to my goals long term
3. I seek honest feedback as often as possible

Answer the following question honestly:

If I keep doing what I am doing today or this week, will I achieve my goal?

Now, let us see in more detail how to approach challenging goals that require complex processes.

How to achieve challenging goals

To reach challenging goals, we must identify:

1. *what* we are trying to accomplish,
2. *why* it matters to us, and
3. *how* we will get there.

Let us look at each point briefly.

1. Identify *what* we are trying to accomplish

How will we know that we have achieved our goals? What are the key success factors?

To accomplish our goals, one of the most important steps—and perhaps the most difficult one—is to set clear goals. The next step is to figure out the key success factors and milestones to hit along the way.

Let us say we want to run a marathon. While it looks like a specific goal, it is not. Is the goal to run a marathon in less than five hours? Is it to be able to run the whole 26.2 miles?

Or is it to cross the finish line even if we have to walk? We will have to adjust our training depending on our goal. To help us be more specific, ask the following question:

How will I know when I have achieved that goal?

In other words, what will the final outcome look like? What would need to happen for us to call it a success?

In truth, most people have vague goals, whether it is losing weight, making money, building a business, or finding a partner. These are not goals, but vague aspirations. Unclear goals lead to poor results.

We must spend time defining our goals in various areas of our lives. We must have enough clarity so that we can visualize the final outcome, not just daydream about it. Once we identify exactly what we are trying to accomplish, we are on the right path to achieving our goals.

* * *

Action step

- Go back to your previous goal.
- Now, make it as specific as you can. Ask yourself the question: "How will I know when I have achieved that goal?"

2. Identify *why* it matters

We pursue goals for a reason. We hope that by achieving

them—or moving toward them—we will experience positive feelings and improve our life. Our "why" is the gasoline we put in our tank to keep going and reach our destination. Without a strong "why", we tend to run out of gas and fail to attain our goals.

Many people would like to get in shape, make more money, or have a more fulfilling career, but their reasons often come from the outside rather than the inside. They focus on what it will get them (respect, fame, wealth, power, etc.), rather than on how it will shape them (character, resilience, compassion, self-respect, etc.). Achieving goals is largely a matter of identity. Unless our goals truly matter to us and become part of our identity, we will struggle to reach them. Ultimately, goals are nothing more than a tool to help us decide who we are or who we aspire to be. They enable us to project ourselves into the future so that we can identify the standard we must set today to end up where we want to be tomorrow.

If our goal is to have a six-pack to impress women at the beach, finding motivation to visit the gym and eat healthily will be difficult. But if we see being healthy as part of who we are and as a sign of self-respect and discipline, hitting the gym regularly will become easier.

If our goal is to make money so that we can buy cool stuff, we might not have enough motivation to go through the countless hardships and the grueling work required to build wealth. But if we see ourselves as a lifelong learner who uses their skills to serve others, we will be more likely to keep going when things get tough—and to eventually make more money.

The point is, identify who you want to be. Then, set your goals accordingly.

* * *

Action step

- Look at your previous goal and reflect on all the reasons you want to reach it.
- Think of what new identity is required of you. Who do you need to be to achieve that goal?

3. Identify *how* to get there

Now that we have identified a clear goal and strong reasons behind it, we must figure out the roadmap to get there. Doing so entails:

1. **Studying successful people.** Look at what people who reached your goals do. What specific process did they rely on? What does their typical day look like? Are there common factors that stand out? Now what could you extrapolate from those data points?
2. **Interviewing people who achieved a similar goal.** Find people who have attained the goal you wish to pursue and interview them. For instance, ask them what they would do differently if they had to start all

over again. Or ask them what they would do if they were in your shoes. Try to get them to elaborate on their strategy and processes. Or look for interviews online.

3. **Educating yourself about your goals.** Read books. Find case studies. Look for effective blueprints. Remember that if something matters to you, you should proactively look for the information you need to reach your goals. That is how you know you are serious.

By studying successful people, interviewing them, and learning more about our goals, we will start getting a sense of what reaching them requires. Once that preliminary work is complete, we should be able to outline an effective blueprint and craft a sound strategy. Once this is done, we must then commit to our goal. Note that major goals will usually require months or years of continuous hard work. Focusing on the process consistently is how to reach them.

Now that we have our roadmap, let us see how we can determine that we are on the right path.

* * *

Action step

To identify the best road map using the action guide, ask yourself:

- Who are the successful people I should study and learn from?

- Who could I interview?
- What books could I read?
- What case studies could I gather?
- What blueprints could I find online?

Gathering feedback

If what we are doing is not going to work, we want to know it early so that we can pivot.

One reason I kept writing self-help books is that I regularly received positive feedback. I was also willing to commit for years, and the market was huge. These factors altogether led me to believe that my odds of success were good enough for me to put in the time and effort. If I had not done this, I might have given up.

The point is, we need to look at our situation objectively and assess whether we are making progress. If we are trying to lose weight, have we managed to shed a few pounds already? If we are learning a foreign language, can we have a basic conversation? If we are practicing the piano, are we able to play a simple piece? If not, have a closer look at our process and figure out what is not working. In short, if our process is effective, we should notice some progress. Although progress may be slow to begin with, it will become obvious over time.

Feedback is the antidote to delusion. The real world will

tell us how we are doing—but we must be willing to listen. Proactively seek feedback. Then, decide whether we should keep going or pivot.

* * *

Action step

- How can you gather more feedback to increase the odds of attaining your goal?

Building the process brick by brick

One common mistake is to want to make big changes immediately, rather than make small changes gradually.

It seldom works.

Achieving major goals is not the result of massive changes made overnight, but of simple habits implemented over time. These habits enable us to build powerful processes that will bring the results we desire.

Here is a typical example of how most of us behave.

First, we see someone who has achieved incredible results. Perhaps, they have the muscular body we aspire to have. Perhaps, they have our dream job. Or perhaps, they have mastered a skill we would love to learn. Then, we logically think, "If I do everything they are doing, I will get the same results". It seems like a reasonable assumption.

The problem is that we just cannot go from A—where *we*

are now—to Z—where *they* are. We cannot skip the entire journey that led them to be where they are today. It likely took them years to implement their current habits and processes. They had to grow into it over time. Therefore, if we mindlessly attempt to copy what they are doing, we will burn out.

Instead, we must start at our own level. We must build our process one brick at a time, at a sustainable pace that works for us. In the end, no process is too complicated. It is just that we have not built the muscles necessary to handle it (yet). Experts may rely on processes that seem "complicated", but for them, it is just what they do. It is part of their identity and, as such, it does not necessarily feel hard. They grew into it—and so can we.

Generally speaking, the more disciplined we are, the more habits we can implement at once. A disciplined person may implement three or four habits at the same time without encountering any problems. On the other hand, a less disciplined person may struggle to stick to just one. But regardless of where we are, we must build our process brick by brick to make it sustainable.

Sadly, we tend to sell ourselves short. That is because we fail to realize how much we can grow. We assume that if we struggle to lift weights, run for more than a couple of minutes, or carry on a basic conversation in a foreign language, we will never reach the level of those people we look up to. While we will definitely struggle on the journey toward our goals, but by building our process over time, we can grow tremendously. In truth, successful people in any field often struggle as much as we do.

- An experienced weightlifter trying to lift their heaviest is not in any more discomfort than a newbie going to the gym for the first time.
- A professional violinist playing a difficult piece is not struggling any more than a beginner touching the violin for the first time.
- A marathon runner attempting to break their personal best might not be suffering more than someone running for the first time in years.

The bottom line is, by building our process over time, we grow while the level of difficulty we face stays more or less constant. The same holds true for most goals. That is why having faith in the process is critical. Achieving extraordinary things is about sticking to the process. What we see as impossible today won't be impossible tomorrow. By starting where we are, building our process one step at a time, and staying consistent over a long enough timeframe, we can attain almost any goal we can envision.

* * *

Action step

- Take a moment to realize that your level of struggle is constant regardless of your starting point. You are not behind or ahead of people. You are exactly where you are supposed to be—right now.

- Think of one habit that if you stick to it daily for months or years would yield exceptional results in the long term.

Assessing results

When pursuing a goal, we may not see results right away. The trick is to figure out whether the process works as soon as possible. Roughly speaking, there are four situations:

1. Effective process and quick progress
2. Effective process but slow progress
3. Ineffective process, but short-term progress
4. Ineffective process and no progress

Let us look at each of these briefly.

1. Effective process and quick progress

This is the best scenario as it enables us to receive positive feedback rapidly. One example would be a training plan that enables us to start gaining strength in a few weeks. Another example would be a lifestyle change that helps us lose weight just a couple of weeks in. Obviously, building muscle or losing weight are goals that will take months and possibly years. But if we notice positive results in the first few weeks, we might be heading in the right direction.

2. Effective progress but slow progress

Sometimes, what we do is effective, but it is not immediately obvious. How do we know if your new skincare routine has any long-term positive effects? What about that business model we are considering implementing?

One solution is to test a process for a specific amount of time. For instance, we can try a language-learning app for a month and see whether we are making progress. If we are not, we can explore other options such as taking private lessons or using another app. I recommend people test a process for two to three weeks at the shortest and three months at the longest. Three months should provide enough time to assess the effectiveness of the process. In the meantime, remember to seek as much feedback as possible.

Another solution, when possible, is to do A/B testing. For instance, apply skin care products on only half of a specific area for three months and see if there is a noticeable difference.

Finally, we can also rely on science or statistics to inform our decisions. For example, we know that excessive sun exposure ages our skin faster. Look at truck drivers. Research has shown that the part of their face closer to the window has significantly more wrinkles. Therefore, we can be confident that applying sunscreen daily will protect our skin against premature aging. Or if we want to invest our money for retirement, look at the historical returns of stock market indexes like the S&P 500. Stats show that by keeping money invested in the S&P 500 for a couple of decades or more, wealth will grow. Knowing those stats can help us keep investing every month, even if the value of our stock portfolio falls in the short term.

Now, while three months is usually enough time to see initial results, there are rare cases where we won't. For example, we may be writing daily on our blog for six months and still have a tiny audience. Or we may be posting on YouTube a couple of times a week for three months and have only a handful of views per video. In those cases, there are two options:

- Keep going, or
- Give up/pivot.

Keep going

Sometimes, we have to keep going without knowing whether our efforts will pay off. If something is important, and/or if we believe the strategy is right, we should give ourselves time. For example, if we want to make YouTube videos, we may choose to commit to doing so for one year. It gives us a timeframe in which to operate knowing that we can quit or reevaluate our strategy in twelve months.

In 2017, when I decided to become a full-time writer, I made the commitment to keep writing for three years. If by April 18th, 2020 (my 35th birthday), things were not going well, I would reevaluate the situation. Every time I became distracted, I reminded myself to refocus on my writing. Interestingly, my writing career took off around April 2020, right at the end of the three years.

The point is, there are times when we must bet on ourselves. Giving ourselves a specific window of time to pursue our goals is an effective way to make progress and avoid giving up too early. It ensures that we don't waste our entire lives travelling down the wrong path while still giving ourselves and our dreams a chance. Of course, it does not mean we should turn our brains off. We should still consider asking the following questions:

- Is my goal specific?
- Is my goal truly important to me, and why? Am I excited about my goal?
- Did I do my best to find the most effective process to reach my goal?
- Am I actively seeking feedback?

In short, as we keep moving toward our goals, we should refine our process and be open to changing direction if necessary.

Give up or pivot

If a goal takes too much time and we cannot seem to see

progress, another option is to give up and choose another goal. Remember that we want our goal to:

- be aligned with our values, mission, and personality, and
- enable us to gather feedback fast so that we can improve.

Some people give up too soon, others keep going when they should have pivoted a long time ago. Truth is, giving up is somewhat of an art. Sometimes, we must be willing to give up on what does not work for us so that we can make room for what will.

3. Ineffective process but short-term progress

A process can be quite ineffective yet enables us to achieve some positive results in the short term. In fact, that is often the case. It is unlikely that by taking consistent action toward our goal, we fail to see at least some progress. The most challenging part is to identify when that process is suboptimal and needs to be improved or replaced with a better one.

For instance, let us say we go to the gym three times a week. At first, we see good gains. It seems like we are heading in the right direction. However, after a while we plateau. We cannot seem to put on muscle or gain strength. That is when we need to refine the process.

One of my friends is an amateur swimmer who competes a few times a year. During his last competition, he was so disappointed with his results that he considered giving up. But, instead, he decided to reevaluate his training. Among other things, he hit the gym and trained specific muscles needed for swimming, reviewed his technique, and worked on building more stamina. As a result, he was able to improve his performance and get his motivation back.

The bottom line is, if we stop making progress, we need to revisit the process and see how we could optimize it. Identify the bottleneck and put in a place a plan to overcome it.

4. Ineffective process and no progress

Finally, a process can be ineffective and waste a great deal of time. If this is the case, we want to know as soon as possible.

For instance, some business models are inherently flawed. In multi-level marketing, only few people at the top of the pile make all the money while everybody else loses. The system is designed so that the vast majority of people cannot be successful. As a result, most people involved in such businesses never make any money despite years of hard work and dedication.

Another example is with "gurus" who sell you courses on how to make money online, whether it is through dropshipping, affiliate marketing, or crypto investing. Many of these courses don't work for a variety of reasons. Here are a few examples:

- The course creator never actually succeeded at that business and does not know what they are talking about.
- The course creator had some past successes, but their business model stopped working, which is why they have pivoted to selling courses.
- The course creator realized that it would be more profitable to sell courses rather than maintain the little bit of success they have had.

Yet another example may be concepts such as the law of attraction. We cannot prove that the law of attraction works, but we cannot completely disprove it either. Thus, while it is a tool we may add to our toolbox, we cannot consider it to be in itself an effective process to reach our goals.

To guard ourselves against ineffective processes, we need to make sure we learn from people who are actually successful. For example, if we want to:

- be fit, learn from people who are actually fit,
- become wealthy, learn from people who are wealthy themselves, and
- go into real estate, learn from people who are actually generating cash flow from properties they own.

Too often, we listen to people who have never done the things we want to do, and this is a bad idea.

To sum up, do whatever is possible to identify the process that enables us to make progress toward our goals. Then, stick to it.

* * *

Action step

- Revisit your previous goal(s).
- Now, for each goal, assess the effectiveness of your process.
- Then, think of what you could change to make your processes more effective.

How to improve your process

Now that we have identified an effective blueprint and started working from it, let us see how we can further improve our process. To refine our process, we can either optimize it or add to it. Let us have a brief look at both options.

Optimizing the process is when we seek to be more efficient in the things we are already doing every day/week.

For example, it is:

- buying better running shoes so that you can run faster,
- improving your techniques at various workout exercises,

- making a healthy recipe tastier, or
- improving the way that you study for exams.

When we optimize, we are merely improving what we are already doing.

On the other hand, *adding to our process* is when we put in place new habits or routines to boost our results and increase the potential to reach our goals. This is when we add to what we are already doing.

For example, it is:

- adding protein to our diet to gain more muscle mass,
- adding another stretch to enhance our flexibility and improve our performance,
- installing an app to track our running performance, or
- hiring a private teacher to help with our language studies.

To simplify, optimizing one's process is *doing better* while adding to one's process is *doing more.* Sometimes, one is more effective than the other. Sometimes, both are necessary. As a rule of thumb, seek to optimize the process first, before adding to it. It is usually more effective and efficient.

Now, look at your current process and ask yourself whether you should optimize it or add to it, and how you could do so.

* * *

Action step

Using your action guide, write down what you could do to optimize your current process and/or add to it.

Putting our process on autopilot

As we keep improving our process, it becomes objectively more complex but subjectively simpler. That is, our brain pays attention to more things and does more work in the background, but it seems easier to us.

For instance:

- an experienced painter has transferred to their subconscious an advanced set of skills that help them create works of art,
- a professional writer has internalized processes that allow them to excel with their words, and
- a seasoned golfer has developed mental representations that enable them to hit the ball almost effortlessly.

In short, for them, what they do seems relatively easy.

When I began writing, I wrote about what interested me and what I thought others would find useful. I wasn't aware of what I was doing wrong or how I could improve my writing. However, over time, I optimized the process, paying attention to a variety of things such as:

- **Logical connections.** Are parts, chapters, or paragraphs connected to each other in a coherent way?
- **Repetitions.** Am I using the same words too many times?
- **Length of sentences.** Are sentences too long or too short?
- **The overall rhythm.** Is the text pleasant to the ear? Does it flow easily?
- **The use of passive forms.** Am I using the passive form excessively?

As I gained experience, I have integrated dozens of factors and gradually improved the process.

* * *

Action step

- What can I do to transfer to my subconscious invaluable skills that will help me reach my goals?

Making the process sustainable

If we implement too many changes at once, we can start to feel overwhelmed. Therefore, it is better to start small and implement only one or two habits at a time.

For instance, to improve our health, we might choose to walk for twenty minutes each day. Once that habit is firmly ingrained, we can add another habit, such as removing sugary drinks from our diet. And once we have managed to get rid of sugary drinks, we could decide to reduce our alcohol consumption.

We are largely creatures of habit. Successful people simply tend to have better habits. What they do each day is aligned with their values and vision. As a result, they are more likely to end up with the kind of life they desire. On the other hand, unsuccessful people often have bad habits. Those habits keep them away from the life they desire.

Slowly adding new habits is how we end up with an elaborate process that works well for us. And that process won't even feel particularly challenging. It is just a matter of building solid habits and growing into the type of person who stays consistent. In fact, our process should *not* feel overly challenging. Otherwise, it would be a sign that it is unsustainable.

Think of a process as a program we install in our brain. At first, we need to code it, which requires time and effort. But once built, it can run on autopilot. I call this "transferring a skill from the conscious to the subconscious". And it is how we progress from undisciplined to disciplined without feeling as though we are doing anything extraordinary. The process is simple. First, we decide what we want to do. Then, we do it consistently until our subconscious takes over. In doing so, we reduce the amount of willpower we need to exert each day. That is how habits work and why they are so powerful.

It is all about starting small and being consistent.

Consistency first, optimization later

To make our process sustainable, we must adopt the following principle:

consistency first, optimization later

In other words, we need to be consistent first before optimizing our process. Build the base of our pyramid by having solid habits. Then, add on top of the solid foundations. Most people fail because the base of their pyramid is shaky. As a result, they cannot build anything on top of it. To avoid being like them, follow the principle of consistency first, optimization later. To do so:

1. **Focus on what matters most.** According to the 80/20 principle, twenty percent of your actions leads to eighty percent of your results. That is, a few of the things we do generate most of our successful outcomes. Therefore, we must make sure that what we choose to do will move the needle in the right direction.

2. **Start small.** The easier it is to start, the more likely we are to act. Therefore, reduce friction. The best way to do so is by starting small.

3. **Stay consistent.** Start small but be consistent. That is how we avoid burning out while making steady progress.

For instance, let us say the goal is to increase our odds of living long and healthy lives. Here is what to do.

1. Focus on what matters most

To live a long and healthy life, most experts agree that people should:

- have a healthy diet,
- avoid smoking avoid alcohol,
- do resistance training (weightlifting, calisthenics, etc.),
- do cardiovascular training, and
- sleep well and for long enough.

Now, to decide where to start, we need to look at our personal situation and consider the following questions:

- What are we struggling with most right now?
- If we were to stick to one habit, which one would have the biggest positive impact on our health?

For example, we could start with exercise, whether it is by going for a run, riding our bike, or swimming twice a week (cardiovascular training). Alternatively, we could lift weights (resistance training).

2. Start small

At first, intensity does not matter. It is all about consistency.

Start small, worry about intensity later.

If we want to run, forget about finding the optimal route, buying the best shoes, or holding the perfect running form. Just buy a decent pair of sneakers and go for a five-minute run twice a week. Do that consistently for a month. Then, slowly increase the intensity and duration over time.

Or if we decide to work out twice a week, just show up at the gym. It is not necessary to train for two hours, lift heavy weights, or drink a pre-workout supplement. The best thing to do is keep it simple.

Remember, there are two main reasons people fail to reach their goals:

1. they never start, or
2. they give up too soon

Avoid these common mistakes by starting small.

As we become comfortable with our habits, over time we can refine them and add new ones.

3. Stay consistent

Consistency enables us to sharpen our skills and optimize our process. It gives us more time to improve and make progress toward our goals.

The problem is that we often have too much on our plates. We are doing too many things at once, or we start projects at an unsustainable pace. As a result, whenever something unexpected happens, the process falls apart and we give up. We simply don't have enough mental bandwidth to deal with everything at once.

That is why it is important to start small. For instance:

- Lift light weights and/or use machines to reduce the risk of injury.
- Dedicate a few minutes to learning a foreign language each day.
- Spend thirty minutes each morning working on a side hustle.

Keep showing up without overextending. There will be plenty of time to optimize the process later. Remember, a process is only powerful to the extent that it can be sustained.

- Writing daily for thirty days might not do much, but writing daily for two years likely will.
- Hitting the gym for one month won't yield impressive results, but working out three times a week for a year probably will.
- Working on a side hustle one hour a day for three months might not generate optimal results, but working on it for three years might.

Consistency is the "magic pill" that activates the power of compounding. It is what turns ordinary people into extraordinary human beings. Without consistency, nothing will work. If we cannot sustain our effort, we will never succeed.

* * *

Action step

- Now, write down how you will apply the principle of "consistency first, optimization later" to reach your goal.
- Then, identify the tasks that matter most, figure out what you will do to start small, and ensure you stay consistent.

Creating a chain of habits

Technically, we can have as many daily processes as we want, but realistically, we want to stick to a few. Even just one process is good to begin with. Then, over time, it is possible to stack more and more habits together to boost results.

For example, start with one daily habit such as:

- writing for fifteen minutes,
- walking for twenty minutes, or
- adding one vegetable or fruit to our diet.

Below are some of the things I am currently doing:

- writing this book,
- going to the gym,
- grabbing a salad on the way home,
- eating my salad, and
- doing some more work.

In short, I have built a solid routine as a way to increase my focus and productivity.

Some people say they don't like routines because they feel restricted. However, the point of having routines is not to constrain us but to give us more time to do what we want outside of those routines. Routines give us more control over our day, they enable us to accomplish more, and, ultimately, they provide us with more freedom to do the things we want. As a rule of thumb, the more processes we can stack together, the better results we will obtain over the long term.

Processes are truly the key to extraordinary results.

* * *

Action step

- Write down two or three powerful habits that you can link together to yield the biggest positive impact over the long term.

- Over time, consider adding more habits and create a chain.

How to focus on the process (in a nutshell)

We have seen what the process is, why it matters, and how to put the right process in place. Now, let us put everything together.

Below is a summary of what to do to focus on the process and reap the associated rewards:

1. **Identify the right process.** Figure out the optimal blueprint to follow to reach our goals. To do so, find role models, interview people, and look for specific plans or methods online.
2. **Start small.** Eliminate friction and make it easy to focus on the tasks that matter each day/week.
3. **Be consistent.** Stick to the process for weeks, months, and even years if needed. Remember, consistency first, intensity later.
4. **Optimize our process.** As consistency becomes part of our identity, gradually optimize the process.
5. **Add to our process.** Make the process more elaborate by adding elements to it, but *only* when/if necessary.
6. **Stack our processes.** Link that process to a new process and rinse and repeat to create a powerful chain of habits.

Focusing on the process is how ordinary people achieve extraordinary things over a long period of time.

It is not easy, but it is simple.

CONCLUSION

As you strive to achieve your goals, many things can go wrong. You may lack motivation. Not all the things you have tried will work. You may doubt yourself. And, like many people, you may give up on the most important goals in your life.

The biggest obstacle will be a lack of consistency. Your inability to stay focused on your goals for long enough will cost you your dreams.

In this book, we have discussed the importance of focusing on the process. We have demonstrated how a simple process followed for a long time will lead to exceptional results. Then, we discussed why we must make the process our main goal, *not* the outcome. Finally, we have seen how to optimize our process to make sure we achieve our goals.

Now, it is up to you to focus on the process and make consistency part of your life. Keep in mind that if consistency has not already transformed your life, then you don't understand it. Embrace consistency and make it part of your identity. It will *inevitably* change your life.

Whenever in doubt, return your focus to the process. Lay the foundations to your success by doing the things that need to be done every day or every week consistently.

Remember that the process is the goal. The outcome you seek is merely its logical consequence. So, keep refocusing on the process as often as necessary until you reach your goals.

The answer to your struggle is almost always to focus on the process.

THIS BOOK IN A NUTSHELL

Here is a brief summary of the main points in this book:

1. **The process is the solution to most of our problems.** The process is what we do each day to enjoy our lives and move closer to our goals. We can never know for sure whether we will reach our goals, but we can always choose to focus on the process. And doing so will enable us to achieve many of our goals.

2. **The process is the goal.** Many people spend a great deal of time and energy worrying about whether they will reach their goals. But the only real goal is not some hypothetical future dream, it is the process we are following right now. In short, the process is the only true goal.

3. **Focusing on the process is all we can ever do.** In

life, there are three types of situations: those we have complete control over, those we have some control over, and those we have no control over. By focusing on the process, we put our attention on what we *can* control while letting go of everything else.

4. **Behind every success, there is a process.** Processes turn ordinary people into extraordinary individuals. No matter how ambitious the goals may be, the way to reach them is to focus on the process. It is to do what is necessary each day consistently at our own pace. We are successful when we follow the process that we believe will enable us to reach our goals.

5. **The process works in all areas.** It is possible to focus on the process to achieve results in any area of life—career, business, relationships, or finance.

6. **The process does not discriminate.** The process does not care about race, gender, or political leaning. While it may vary based on an individual's personal situation, there is always a process that can help.

7. **Finding the right process is an art.** Sometimes, the process is straightforward, other times, not so much. Finding the right process will often require us to do our own research. In some cases, it will be more of an art than a science.

8. **Consistency is key.** First and foremost, be consistent.

Build simple habits first and only add to them later. This will prevent us from feeling overwhelmed or worried. Remember this: "consistency first, optimization later".

9. **Faith matters.** Faith is believing even when there is no reason to. Learn how to trust the process even when short-term results are disappointing or nonexistent. In many ways, everyone needs to have faith.

ACTION GUIDE

Part I. What the process is and why it matters

Select one major goal you have achieved in the past. My goal was:

____

____

____

Then, answer the following questions:

What was the process that enabled me to reach my goals? What was I doing each day/week?

____

____

____

____

What were the benefits? Rate yourself on each of them below:

Benefit #1. It reduced my stress, worry, and my sense of overwhelm.

1____10

Benefit #2. It boosted my emotional resilience.

1____10

Benefit #3. It enhanced my focus.

1____ 10

Benefit #4. It strengthened my self-discipline.

1____ 10

Benefit #5. It compounded my results.

1____ 10

Benefit #6. It put the focus back on myself.

1____ 10

Part II. How to focus on the process

A. Prioritize process goals over result goals

Select one goal you want to work on. Then, follow steps 1 to 4 below:

- Step 1—Set a clear target
- Step 2—Break it down into milestones
- Step 3—Put in place the right process
- Step 4—Focus on the process

Step 1—Set a clear target

Write down your specific goal below. Make sure it is as specific as possible.

My goal:

____

____

____

Step 2—Break it down into milestones

Identify at least three main milestones you will need to reach along the way:

1. ______________________________________

____

2. ______________________________________

____

3. ______________________________________

____

Step 3—Put in place the right process

Try to identify a couple of habits or actions you could take each day to make progress toward your goal in the coming weeks and/or months.

What my process could look like:

____

Step 4—Focus on the process

Once you have identified your process, practice focusing on it so that you get some of the six benefits mentioned in part one (stress reduction, emotional resilience, focus, self-discipline, compound effect, inner focus).

B. Understand the cycle of excitement

Think of a time you entered the cycle of excitement with one of your goals.

Write down the specific goal I have in mind:

Reflect on what happened. Did you keep going? Did you give up? What could you have done differently, if anything?

What happened:

C. Develop faith in the process

How much time do you spend worrying about the results? Rate yourself below:

My overall level of worry

1____ 10

Now, is it helping you reach your goals? If yes, how? If not, why is that?

D. Realize that the process is the goal

Take a moment to reflect on the fact that your process will lead you to the achievement of your goals.

Then, visualize yourself making progress toward your goals each day—forever. Consider the following question:

What will likely happen in the next six months, twelve months, five years, and ten years, if I stay consistent, keep going, and refuse to give up?

____

____

____

E. Clarify your goals

Revisit your previous goal in *A. Prioritize process goals over result goals.*

Now, how could you make it even more specific and create a better process?

My previous goal:

____

____

What could you do to make it more specific and improve the process?

____

____

____

____

F. Start small

If you were to do something consistently, for at least six months, which small action(s) would enable you to make progress toward your goals with almost one hundred percent certainty?

My small action(s):

____

____

____

____

G. Make consistency part of your identity

Think of consistency as part of who you are. Tell yourself that you are someone who is extremely consistent. You always keep focusing on the process until you reach your goals.

Adopt the following mantra:

"I keep going until I reach my goals. It is just who I am."

Alternatively, come up with your own mantra.

H. Commit to a thirty-day challenge

Revisit your previous goal.

Then, select one habit to stick to for the next thirty days as part of your challenge.

My one habit:

____

I. Practice self-compassion

1. Reassess your belief around self-compassion and let go of the following myths:

   Myth #1. Self-compassion is selfish

   Myth #2. Being kind to yourself is a sign of weakness

   Myth #3. Self-compassion will make you lazy

2. Monitor your self-talk

This week, pay extra attention to the way you talk to yourself. Write down examples of what you say to yourself in the following instances:

- When you make a mistake
- When something does not go as planned
- When you experience negative emotions such as frustration, anger, jealousy, or sadness

My self-talk when I make a mistake:

____

____

____

____

My self-talk when things don't go as planned:

____

____

____

____

My self-talk when I experience negative emotions:

____

____

____

____

3. Update your self-talk

Now, write down what you would like to say to yourself instead: My positive self-talk when I make a mistake:

____

____

____

____

My positive self-talk when things don't go as planned:

____

____

____

____

My positive self-talk when I experience negative emotions:

____

____

____

____

Part III. Refining your process

Identifying the right process

Revisit your previous goals. Now, rate yourself on the three points below:

I learn anything I can about my goals

1____10

I am willing to commit to it long term

1____10

I seek honest feedback as often as possible

1____10

Answer the following question honestly:

If I keep doing what I am doing today or this week, will I achieve my goal?

How to achieve challenging goals

1. Identify *what* you are trying to accomplish

Go back to your previous goal.

Now, make it as specific as you can. To do so, answer the following question:

How exactly will I know I have achieved that goal? My answer:

2. Identify *why* it matters to you

Look at your previous goal and reflect on all the reasons you want to reach it.

The main reasons I want to reach my goal:

1.
2.
3.
4.
5.

Think of what new identity is required of you. Who do you need to be to achieve that goal? To achieve that goal, I need to adopt the identity of someone who:

3. Identify *how* you will get there

Identify the best road map by answering the following questions:

Who are the successful people I should study and learn from?

____

____

____

Who could I interview?

____

____

What books could I read? What blueprints could I find online? What case studies could I gather?

____

____

____

Gathering feedback

How could you gather more feedback so that you can increase the odds of attaining your goal?

____

Building your process brick by brick

Take a moment to realize that your level of struggle is constant regardless of your starting point. You are not behind or ahead of people. You are exactly where you are supposed to be *right now*.

Write down one skill you learned and mastered:

Now, reflect on the initial struggle and the current struggle. Is there a difference? Would you say it was harder when you got started or that it is harder now?

Finally, think of one habit that if you stick to it daily for months or years would yield exponential results in the long term. Write it down below:

Assessing your results

Processes fall mostly into one of the four categories below:

1. Effective process and quick progress
2. Effective process but slow progress
3. Ineffective process, but short-term progress
4. Ineffective process and no progress

Revisit your previous goal.

Now, assess the effectiveness of your process for that specific goal (up until now). Rate yourself using the scale below:

1____10

Comments, if any:

____

____

____

Then, think of what you could change to make your process more effective. Write your answer below:

____

____

____

____

How to improve your process

Write down what else you could do to optimize your current process and/or add to it.

I could optimize my process by:

____

____

____

I could add to my process by:

____

____

____

Putting your process on autopilot

What could you do to transfer to your subconscious invaluable skills that will help you reach your goals?

____

____

____

Making your process sustainable

Remember the following concept:

Consistency first, optimization later

To help you apply that principle in your life, make sure you:

1. focus on what matters most,
2. start small, and
3. stay consistent.

Now, write down how you will apply the principle of "consistency first, optimization later" to reach your goal.

For my specific goal, consistency first, optimization later means:

____

____

____

Creating a chain of habits

Write down two or three powerful habits that if you were to link together would yield the biggest positive impact over the long term.

Habit #1:

Habit #2:

Habit #3:

Over time, consider adding more habits to create a solid chain of habits.

OTHER BOOKS BY THE AUTHOR

Mastery Series

1. Master Your Emotions: A Practical Guide to Overcome Negativity and Better Manage Your Feelings
2. Master Your Motivation: A Practical Guide to Unstick Yourself, Build Momentum and Sustain Long-Term Motivation
3. Master Your Focus: A Practical Guide to Stop Chasing the Next Thing and Focus on What Matters Until It is Done
4. Master Your Destiny: A Practical Guide to Rewrite Your Story and Become the Person You Want to Be
5. Master Your Thinking: A Practical Guide to Align Yourself with Reality and Achieve Tangible Results in the Real World
6. Master Your Success: Timeless Principles to Develop Inner Confidence and Create Authentic Success
7. Master Your Beliefs: A Practical Guide to Stop Doubting Yourself and Build Unshakeable Confidence
8. Master Your Time: A Practical Guide to Increase Your Productivity and Use Your Time Meaningfully

9. Master Your Learning: A Practical Guide to Learn More Deeply, Retain Information Longer and Become a Lifelong Learner
10. Master Your Potential: A Practical Guide to Break Free from Limitations and Start Tapping Into Your Greatness
11. Master Your Decisions: A Practical Guide to Make Better Decisions Faster and Stack the Odds in Your Favor

Productivity Series

1. Dopamine Detox: A Short Guide to Remove Distractions and Get Your Brain to Do Hard Things
2. Immediate Action: A 7-Day Plan to Overcome Procrastination and Regain Your Motivation
3. Powerful Focus: A 7-Day Plan to Develop Mental Clarity and Build Strong Focus
4. Strategic Mindset: A 7-Day Plan to Identify What Matters and Create a Strategy that Works

Other books

Do the Impossible: How to Become Extraordinary and Impact the World at Scale

Essays to Change Your Life: Think Better, Act Smarter, Work With Meaning

Do What Works for You: A Practical Guide to Align Your Actions with Your Authentic Self

ABOUT THE AUTHOR

THIBAUT MEURISSE

Thibaut is the author of over 20 books including the #1 Amazon Bestseller, "Master Your Emotions" which has sold over 500,000 copies and has been translated into more than 30 languages including French, Spanish, German, Chinese, Thai, and Portuguese.

Thibaut's mission is to help ordinary people attain extraordinary results.

If you like simple, practical, and inspiring books, and are committed to improve your life, you will love his work.

thibautmeurisse.com thibaut.meurisse@gmail.com